D1636238

HOW TO BE UNSTOPPABLE
THROUGH THE NINE STAR SOCIAL VALUES

STAR POWER

MIKE LIPKIN

Star Power: How To Be Unstoppable Through The Nine Star Social Values
© 2013 Mike Lipkin

First Edition 2013

Environics/Lipkin Inc.
33 Bloor Street East, Suite 1020
Toronto Ontario
Canada M4W 3H1

ISBN 978-0-9732958-4-9
Design and layout by Sarah Battersby

Printed in Canada

START NOW.
NEVER END.

MIKE LIPKIN was raised in South Africa. He immigrated to Toronto, Canada in 2001 but he left all his baggage behind.

He is the founder and chief partner of Environics/Lipkin, the motivation company that has inspired over a million people in 43 countries. Someone, somewhere close to you, is raising their game because of Environics/Lipkin.

Mike lives to talk and he talks to live. His personal mission is to give people the insights that excite them into powerful action. In 2012, he delivered 150 programs internationally to clients that included Deloitte, DHL, Merck, Pfizer, Procter & Gamble, GE, Wells Fargo, BMW and Tata Communications.

This is Mike's fourteenth book. In line with his philosophy that life is theatre with consequences, he promises to entertain you while you learn. Enjoy.

CONTENTS

Star: Someone who thrives on change and instability; someone who grows in direct proportion to the challenges facing her; someone who proves it can be done; someone who is a model of what's possible.

Star Social Value: A force that drives us at our core. It determines the way we feel, think, and interact with others and ultimately, what we become. It evolves slowly over time or it can develop suddenly in response to dramatic events. It enables preeminent performance against all odds.

I have long argued that, because of enormous leaps in technology, the values we hold are coming into question. More than ever before, we need to step back and consciously design our lives. We need to decide explicitly what we stand for and whether we are the slave or the master of the new technology.

~Don Tapscott
The Globe And Mail
March 23, 2013

DO YOU KNOW HOW GOOD YOU REALLY ARE?

Here's the question that we ask ourselves most often: Do I have what it takes? And here's our answer: I don't know.

After motivating almost a million people in 43 countries over the past 20 years, there is one truth that I have learned: Even the highest achievers are plagued by self-doubt. Their external confidence masks an internal fear, "One day, people will find out that I'm not good enough."

> Fear is a universal emotion. It's a primitive drive that is vital to survival. It's a superb servant but a shocking master.

Sound familiar? Welcome to being human. Fear is a universal emotion. It's a primitive drive that is vital to survival. It's a superb servant but a shocking master. Too little fear leads to personal complacency and obsolescence. Too much fear suffocates our spirit and saps our energy. Just the right amount of fear sharpens our senses and adrenalizes our actions.

This program will inspire you with just the right amount of fear. You will learn how the most successful people achieve amazing results against all odds and how they sustain their preeminence throughout their lifetime. You will be reminded of why you are great. You will be awakened to ideas that will make you greater. And you will be moved to do things that you've never done before.

The most valuable people in our lives are the ones that make us happy. They thrill us with their love, their mastery, their energy, their creativity and their generosity. When we think of them, we light up from the inside out.

My mission is to thrill you with insights so you can thrill others. I want to share the wows and the wisdom I have harvested over a lifetime of coaching and motivating others. I want you to get the good stuff fast so you can make people happy.

In 2001, I emigrated from Johannesburg, South Africa to Toronto, Canada. I formed a partnership with Environics, one of Canada's leading research companies. I chose Environics because of their marvelous tool – the Social Values Monitor.

Launched in 1983, the Social Values Monitor tracks and analyzes the evolution of social values and beliefs across Canada and the United States. It also enables clients to link national research with parallel research from 20 countries around the world.

This rich, innovative methodology has helped hundreds of top companies understand their customers and employees more deeply, and tailor their communications to better connect with their stakeholders' core values. You can find out more by visiting **www.environics.ca**

To identify The Nine Star Social Values I have distilled and combined Environics data with my personal experience. The Nine Star Social Values are the inner-resources that make the Great Ones great. They are simple to understand but not as simple to execute.

When the star is ready, inspiration strikes. You're ready. That's why you're reading this. It's your time to thrive. I know The Nine Star Social Values will expand your capacity to create remarkable results. I'm excited for you because when you succeed, I win.

DESIGNED TO INSPIRE & ACTIVATE YOU

I want *Star Power* to become your personal handbook for success. I also want it to be a fabulous learning experience for you.

It begins with a simple nine-question survey to evaluate where you are in your integration of The Nine Star Social Values.

Then I define each Star Social Value. My insights are written as a series of independent mantras that can be understood at a glance. I have stripped away any verbiage that gets in the way of your immediate understanding.

There are over 500 mantras in this book. Any one of them is powerful enough to be your key takeaway and primary inspiration. Highlight the ones that are most meaningful to you.

As you explore each mantra, write down your reflections in the margin and the spaces provided. By the time you've finished the book, I want you to have written almost as many mantras as I have.

To conclude the exploration of each Star Social Value, I have offered you three opportunities to develop your mastery in this space. Invest the time to write down your thoughts. Be spontaneous. Sometimes your first responses are your authentic responses. You can always change them later. Share them with friends and colleagues. Talk is a powerful agent of change.

Finally, share your thoughts with me so we can take this conversation wherever it needs to go. www.mikelipkin.com

ARE YOU A STAR?

Here's a simple test to evaluate your personal integration of the Star Social Values. On a scale of 1-10 (1 = lowest, 10 = highest), rate your spontaneous response to the following statements. It takes 9 to be a Star:

1.	I often do something just to prove to myself that I am able to do it:	☐
2.	I see complexity and change as learning experiences and sources of opportunity:	☐
3.	I am able to fully express my talent and personality to others:	☐
4.	I am able to control my emotions so they enable me to succeed in any situation:	☐
5.	I focus on eating, exercise and self-transformation to create a healthy life:	☐
6.	I am searching for meaning and a higher purpose to my life that transcends my day-to-day activities:	☐
7.	I like to be part of social networks and communities where people are deeply connected:	☐
8.	I consider myself as much a citizen of the world as I am a citizen of my own country:	☐
9.	I feel secure and confident that that my financial resources enable me to live the life that's right for me:	☐

For a deeper exploration of
The Nine Star Social Values
and what they mean to you
personally, go to
www.mikelipkin.com/starpower
and type in the code STAR999
to discover how evolved you
are on each Star Social Value.

THE NINE STAR SOCIAL VALUES

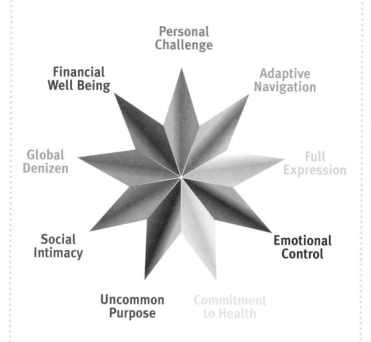

Personal
Challenge

Financial
Well Being

Adaptive
Navigation

Global
Denizen

Full
Expression

Social
Intimacy

Emotional
Control

Uncommon
Purpose

Commitment
to Health

PERSONAL CHALLENGE:

The core belief that once one sets oneself a goal, one will achieve it; commitment to finishing what one starts; continually setting oneself difficult goals in order to grow; perception of problems and predicaments as offers to be embraced; a blend of optimism and appetite that keeps one happy and hungry in equal measure; belief that everything leads to ultimate success.

MANTRA

"I'm Ready. Bring It On."

PERSONAL CHALLENGE

■ Don't look to your horoscope, look to yourself.

••

■ Don't listen to the idiot in your head who says it can't be done. Listen to the genius that says it can be done and the doer that says go do it.

••

■ The wise person does now what the fool does eventually. Procrastinate later, do it now. Our mental muscles expand in direct proportion to the challenges given to them.

••

■ Success means being preeminent. Preeminent means becoming the benchmark for others. As Martin Luther King Jr. said, "If it falls to your lot to be a street sweeper, sweep streets like Michelangelo painted pictures, sweep streets like Beethoven composed music, sweep streets like Shakespeare wrote poetry."

••

MY MANTRAS

_____

_____

_____

_____

_____

■ **The quality of your life is not what appears on the scoreboard.** The quality of your life is really who you're being while you play the game. The scoreboard measures excellence. Without the scoreboard, there can be no excellence but you don't win the game by looking at the scoreboard. Yet, sometimes we're so intimidated by the scoreboard that we don't even look at it. But if you don't check the scoreboard, you don't know what action to take. See the number on the scoreboard and be committed to changing it.

■ **Whatever we look for is what we tend to find.** If we're not even sure what we're looking for, we'll find *FUD* – fear, uncertainty and doubt. Focus is powerful. And energy is at its strongest where and when it's concentrated. So if we know exactly what we want, we may just find it.

MY MANTRAS

■ **What motivates people to take on challenges and evolve to the next level?** How do certain people become champions on demand? It's a moment of awakening. It's when we recognize that something must be done and we must do it. Our *must do* enables our *can do*. We find or make a way. Our determination is self-fulfilling. And we realize that we are capable of doing so much more.

··

■ **We act out the image we have of ourselves.** So we have to build our identity as leaders and influencers. Mastery is about self-definition and self-control. We cannot manage what we do not understand.

··

■ **People crave people and things that are proven and dependable.** They want a guarantee of results in a future that offers precisely the opposite. For the time being, the easy times are over. Now, it's serious, and serious times demand substance.

··

MY MANTRAS

_____

_____

_____

_____

_____

■ Smart people understand that we cannot simplify issues beyond a certain level. There is no instant panacea or formula for immediate success. Call it the new irony: technology enables us to do more things quicker. Yet it takes more time with more people to get things done. That's because at a certain threshold, it's about blood, sweat and tears. It's about picking up the phone, having the meetings, creating alliances, building trust, complying with regulations, and going the distance.

MY MANTRAS

■ **The Old Guys (and Gals) are back.** There is a huge need for a calm mind and a still heart in the turbulence and chaos. There is a huge relief in being around someone who has shown that they can navigate the crisis and bring us safely to our destination. There is huge merit in having stood the test of time.

■ **Integrity, authenticity and courage are back in fashion.**

■ **Be frequently in error, but never in doubt.** Never waver, never wobble. When you discover you've made a mistake, declare your lessons and move forward with conviction. Don't retreat, refine and move on. Bravado breaks down barriers.

■ **"Waffle House has a very simple operational philosophy: Get Open.** They never close. If there is a storm, they try to get their stores open. It doesn't matter if they don't have power or gas. If they can get a generator in there, they'll get going. They'll make coffee with bottled water." ~ *Craig Fugate, head of Federal Emergency Management Agency*

■ If all anyone ever said about you was that "you always deliver on your promises," it may be enough to make you indispensable to them.

. . . .

■ **Even decades come in twenty-four hour packages.** We can do it all, we just cannot do it all at once.

. . . .

■ **When one is eye-to-eye with the tiger, one cannot be distracted.** That may be our greatest challenge: to switch off the noise and find power in the silence within.

. . . .

■ **Play offense with the future, not defense with the past.** Imagine what can be done with what you have, then do it. Don't be concerned with the odds against you. The Force is with you.

. . . .

MY MANTRAS

_____

_____

_____

_____

_____

_____

_____

_____

31

■ When you declare your intentions to others and they hold you to account, it gets you moving faster.

■ Success is the result of following through on your commitment after the mood in which you made the commitment expired.

■ "Contrary to widespread public opinion, a considerable proportion of New Year resolvers do succeed. You are 10 times more likely to change by making a New Year's resolution compared to non-resolvers with identical goals and comparable motivation to change." ~ *Dr John Norcross, psychologist, University of Scranton*

■ No matter how many times someone has said NO to you, ask them again. They're not the same person and neither are you. Things change. People change. Possibilities change.

MY MANTRAS

■ **Believe without proof**. We know what we have to do and we do it. Our determination overcomes our doubt. We trust our inner superpower to pole-vault past our difficulties. We're ready to be both amazed and amazing. By increasing the size of our hearts, we win the hearts of others. Courage takes you past the point that preparation takes you to. It's where fear meets integrity.

■ **Difficulty wakes up genius.**

MY MANTRAS

■ **When you don't do what you know you must do, it prevents you from doing anything else.** Why is that? Because you're constantly thinking about what you should have done and haven't done. It interferes with every other activity. It's the discordant thought that gets in the way of the masterpiece. You know it. Other people feel it. And the more you procrastinate, the more discordant the thought becomes. Sometimes it becomes so discordant, it's painful. And that's where the great decision must be made: do nothing and succumb to it or take action and resolve it.

• •

■ **I see it all the time: people who have resigned themselves to do less because they've lost the will to do more**. How about you? What have you put off? Where have you drifted? How have you let yourself down? Think about it. This could be a defining moment for you. It's the moment you choose effort and application over inertia and regret. It's the moment you reclaim your self-purpose over self-pity. Maybe most importantly, rather than disappear into the darkness, it's the moment you shine a light for others.

• •

■ **Fear of failing is one of the biggest causes of failure.** Focus on the game. Trust in the outcome. It may be different to what you expected, but it's always what it is meant to be.

• •

■ **Failure is never failure unless you become the failure.** What do I mean? Failure is always an event. It's a result you didn't want, but it may be exactly the result you need. Read the signs right and you will be all right.

• •

■ My biggest successes have come from my biggest "failures," including six months of clinical depression 21 years ago that inspired me to become a motivator.

• •

■ **It's only when you say the fatal words, "I am a failure,"** that your prediction will come true. Don't blame anything or anyone with peace of mind again. Whatever happens to you is an offer that life is making you. Accept it as a gift.

• •

MY MANTRAS

_____

_____

_____

_____

_____

■ **The difference between right and wrong is often miniscule.** The best thing to do is the right thing to do. The next best thing is the wrong thing. Every action creates its own momentum. If you act with courage and conviction, the world will conspire with you to succeed.

....

■ **The mark of today's winners isn't grounded solely in data, it's about personal confidence.** Too much is changing all the time for anyone to be fully backed by the facts. Big steps require huge leaps of faith.

....

■ **The more you try, the more you learn.** Endure the inevitable frustration, annoyance, irritation, fatigue, blues and tension as you experiment with new media and ideas. Be resilient. The comfort zone is the antithesis of preeminence. We can only lead others where we are prepared to go. Go first, even if you slip, stumble and fall. That's still progress. Resilience is bouncing back with even more verve and passion.

....

■ **Who you are right now is created by the future you are living into.** Understand the crisis paradox: in tough times, the majority of people tend to lose their optimism and energy. They are worn down by their anxieties. Their desire to thrive is replaced by their need to survive. The demand for bold aggressive action is greater, but because the supply is smaller, bold aggressive operators are highly rewarded.

....

■ **It's election time, and I'm not talking federal politics.** Today is Election Day. Surprise, surprise: every day is Election Day. 24 hours is the new term of office.

....

MY MANTRAS

_____

_____

_____

_____

_____

_____

_____

_____

_____

_____

_____

■ Are you content to just carry on? Or do you want to see how far you can go? Do you seek the safety of the herd? Or are you willing to live on the tipping point?

• •

■ **Whoever you are, someone is counting on you to go first.** Someone is looking to you for inspiration. Someone needs your contribution right now. Be the person that helps others be the best version of themselves.

• •

■ "Comfort the afflicted and afflict the comfortable." ~ *Kevin Conroy*

■ **Be a candidate for what's possible.** Give people something to rally around. You can be idealistic and realistic at the same time. It may even be mandatory for success. Be the reason why someone does something they would never otherwise have done.

■ Seize the moment or you might seize up in the moment.

■ **Be unflappable.** Extraordinary people stay centered in the chaos. Crises are their finest moments.

MY MANTRAS

_____

_____

_____

_____

_____

_____

_____

_____

_____

_____

■ **Back yourself when your back is against the wall.** You'll find that others have got your back as well.

....

■ Don't have your nervousness be the reason that you don't step up.

....

■ It's ok to be afraid but don't let it stop you.

....

■ **In stripped-down organizations, the individual is decisive.** The bigger the scale, the more important every interaction becomes. Whether it's a law firm or an airline, the individual is the ambassador of the company and the company is judged by the individuals it keeps.

....

■ **Confidence is constructed from consciousness.** It is the bridge from safe to scary. It's about trusting oneself and others. It's belief translated into action. It's going where you haven't been before even though you don't know the way. Confidence is your Teflon skin that protects you against self-doubt. It means never backing down when you know you need to back yourself. It's the gift you give yourself. And it's the gift no one can take away.

....

■ **Confidence needs humility** to save it from becoming obstinacy. The distance between hero and zero can be horribly short. Humility means believing in yourself but not your self-importance.

. . . .

■ **If courage is at the core of our character, confidence is at the edge.** Confidence is courage out loud. It means expressing our courage so others can follow. It's the quality that is most visible. That's why it's so vital.

. . . .

■ **Confidence precedes competence because it attracts competence.** On the other hand, competence without confidence goes unused. It breaks my heart to witness the number of highly competent people who are leaving their skills on the table because they're too afraid to fail.

. . . .

MY MANTRAS

■ The real danger is not that we set our targets too high and miss them. It's that we set them too low and hit them.

••

■ Do the things you don't want to do so you can be the person that you've always wanted to be.

••

■ FLAP – Finish Like A Pro.

••

MY MANTRAS

MY PERSONAL GOALS:

Set yourself three personal goals to be achieved in the next 12 months. Each one should both stretch and inspire you to go where you've never gone before.

MY IRRESISTIBLE OFFERS:

Identify three problem areas that cannot be avoided and discern why they are great opportunities to grow. Then evaluate the best way for you to respond to them. Experiment with your approaches.

ULTIMATE SUCCESS MEANS:

Define what ultimate success means to you. What will it take for you to achieve personal fulfillment and self-actualization? How can you keep moving towards it?

ADAPTIVE NAVIGATION

The capacity to adapt oneself to life's uncertainties and change; the desire to explore complexity as a learning experience and source of opportunity; the understanding that complexity is the antithesis of neat and tidy; the ability to focus on what counts while seeing the bigger picture; the ability to go fast and slow.

MANTRA

"Life's a magical mystery and I'm going to solve it."

ADAPTIVE NAVIGATION

■ **Life is a game that we all play.** Playing a game without knowing the rules is like flying blind. We tend to crash into things.

....

■ **The key to personal power is having fewer rules and living by them.**

....

■ **We only know that we understand when we can help someone else know and understand.** Until we master our communication, we may be speaking a language that's foreign to everyone else. What other people hear may not be what we say. Until we can speak our thoughts in a way that others can understand, we cannot be sure we understand.

....

■ **While you read this, you're changing.** We know we're growing older but we can't see ourselves from inside our own heads. Even the face we see in the mirror isn't the face that others see. Everything is an interpretation by someone else.

....

■ **Success means seeing the change *and* being the change.**

....

■ **If you ever say that you've arrived, you're dead.** You're only as good as how you're being *at the moment.*

. . . .

■ **Seeing the change means recognizing the pattern and projecting it into the future.** There is a logic and rhythm to everything. Every change is either an extension of the pattern or a disruption of it. We need to step back enough to recognize the pattern but be close enough to see the details of it.

. . . .

■ **We need to zoom out, then we need to zoom in.** And we need to know when to do what.

. . . .

■ **If you don't invest in your future, you won't thrive there.** Life is a three-act play. Yesterday was our first act. Today is our second act. Tomorrow is our third act. "What's past is pro-logue," said Shakespeare. Tomorrow, today will be yesterday. What you do today is who you will become tomorrow. What kind of day are you going to make it?

. . . .

MY MANTRAS

_____

_____

_____

■ *Genchi Genbutsu* – the motto of Toyota, means "go and see" what the cause of the problem is. Don't rely on second hand reports.

....

■ We are all part of the change process. Whether we are mere observers or primary movers of change, our presence influences what happens next. The observer affects what is being observed but the mover shapes it.

....

■ Ignorance isn't bliss; it's pain that's been delayed. Colliding with a reality for which you're not prepared can kill you.

....

■ In all our research, people are asking three big questions: Firstly, they are asking: what is really going on? Secondly, they are asking: what is going to happen? Thirdly, they are asking: What should I do?

....

■ Be prepared. Success is where the future meets a mind that is ready for it.

....

■ Consume a media diet designed to keep you vital, informed and inspired.

....

■ **Once you've consumed your media, you need to format it.** No matter what you do for a living, you're in the business of packaging and merchandizing information. How you format your information determines how much of it others want to consume. The method is the message.

■ **Knowledge of the trends is like mental radar.** It endows you with the power of anticipation so you can maximize your success rate. The future leaves clues. If you know what you're looking for, you can see a lot.

MY MANTRAS

■ **Open your eyes – we are all subject to willful blindness where we choose not to see what's staring at us.** We're also subject to "confirmational bias" where we only see what affirms our beliefs or past.

....

■ **When we evolve slower than our external environment, we lose our relevance and value.** When we evolve ahead of our environment, we become distinctive and desirable to others.

....

■ **We all want to be with people who anticipate and act on problems before they occur, or at least before they become crises.** How about you? What's your anticipate-react record? Are you ahead of the curve or behind the eight ball?

....

■ **Anyone can have an excellent game.** Only champions have game excellence. The marketplace demands the best all the time. Commercial love is always conditional on the goods we bring to every encounter.

....

■ **Context is everything.** The trends will sweep us along whether we're aware of them or not. Success without awareness is called luck. It's a one-time or sometime thing. On the other hand, success generated by awareness is called "informed action" and it yields superior, sustained results.

....

■ "It's all about maximizing collisions and accelerating serendipity." ~ *Tony Hsieh, CEO, Zappos*

....

MY MANTRAS

■ **The three principles of the African wild: Imperfection is perfection.** Asymmetry is symmetry. Nothing is fair but everything is balanced.

· ·

■ **We're all operating in a tighter space.** Either we play by the rules or we're disqualified from playing. It's not good enough just knowing the rules, we have to embrace them. Going rogue is not an option. But neither is resigned submission. The greater the constraints, the more creative we need to be.

· ·

■ **Complexity tends to hide the secrets of success.** Great ventures come from constant and neverending effort and application. The grind is the message. It can either sharpen us or crush us.

· ·

■ **You cannot be great if you live in a small world.** You need to inhabit the biggest world that is open to you.

· ·

■ **The more we know, the more we realize that we don't know.** And the more inspired we become to find out more. The more questions we ask, the more motivated we become to ask more.

· ·

■ Sometimes we need to go too far to know how far we can go.

• •

■ **Life has a way of dealing with people who don't respect boundaries.** It either destroys them or salvages them, depending on how fast they change their ways.

• •

■ **Rules are there to keep us safe and ensure the game is fair and playable.** But too many rules obstruct freedom and possibility. Our challenge is to discern what rules to follow, what rules to ignore and what rules to change.

• •

■ **Learn to love the idiots in your life because in someone else's life, you're the idiot.** And by the way, an idiot may be anyone who doesn't play by the same rules that you do. Success means being great with idiots.

• •

MY MANTRAS

_____

_____

_____

_____

_____

_____

_____

_____

■ **Making others wrong, doesn't make things better.**

■ **There is a level at which everything is metaphorical.** The word comes from the ancient Greek word "metaphora," which means, "carry across or over." It's when things become symbols or emblems of something else. That means everything has a meaning that's bigger than its literal translation.

■ **Our lives are enriched when we open ourselves up to metaphors.** It means there is a world beyond the face value of the thing or experience. For example, have you ever branded someone as an angel? Or have you ever told someone they're a godsend? Or have you looked at your first coffee of the day and thought of it as life-saving nectar? Or considered the first cold beer at the end of a hot summer's day as liquid gold?

■ **We're all metaphors in other people's minds.** We all stand for something beyond who we are as flesh, blood, and bone. What do you stand for in others' minds?

■ Life is full of "binary moments" – go or stop, launch or cancel, love or leave, buy or sell. Sometimes, it could get messy but inside the mess is the message. Ultimately, it will work out if you do the hard work. Inertia is not your friend. Choose and act.

■ Act like the next big storm is coming soon. That doesn't mean running scared. It means being super prepared. It means being so prepared that others turn to us for guidance and safety.

MY MANTRAS

■ **Whatever happens next, it's going to be extreme.** It's going to be exhausting. It's going to take deep personal reservoirs of stamina and resilience. So build your capacity now. Train your mind and body to be ready. There is a gym near you waiting for you to register. There are presentations and ideas waiting to be developed. There are people waiting to collaborate and connect with you. Now is a good time to get going.

■ **Anything is obvious once it's been thought of.** The most successful breakthroughs always appear to be self-evident once they've been introduced. How many times have you exclaimed "I knew it!" or "I thought of that!" when you've been confronted with The Next Big Thing?

■ **Earn face-time with others by making it a great time.** Alone time is important but together time is priceless. The person with the richest perspective makes the best choices and nothing produces perspective like great conversations with great people.

■ **In the new flat, multigenerational, multicultural, digital, postmodern reality, no one can order anyone to do anything.** Autocratic environments don't even work in the military any more. The new currencies of success are consensus and connection. This is the age of apocalyptic anxiety and explosive opportunity in equal measure. The newest member of the team is just as likely to be the greatest source of wisdom as the oldest.

....

■ **Flow freely.** Comfort zones are for wimps. We need to morph into whatever the market demands. The past is merely the platform for future success. Whoever travels light, travels farthest. The fast eat the slow. We're all going where we've never been before. It's a thrilling ride.

....

MY MANTRAS

_____

_____

_____

_____

_____

_____

_____

_____

_____

■ **Hold on tight and be prepared to let go at any time.** We all have built-in parachutes.

....

■ **Touch The Ground Lightly.** Embrace the temporary. Say "yes" to impermanence and portability.

....

■ **"The European Union is cracking up.** The Arab world is cracking up. China's growth model is under pressure and America's credit-driven capitalist model has suffered a warning heart attack and needs a total rethink. Recasting any one of these alone would be huge. Doing all four at once — when the world has never been more interconnected — is mind-boggling. We are again 'present at the creation'—but of what?" ~ *Thomas Friedman*

....

■ **Look at your life through fresh eyes.** Imagine you were someone new coming into your world. What would they see that you're not seeing? What surprises would they find that may currently be hidden from your view? Why would they love being you? What are you taking for granted that would delight them? Perspective is a view from a place where you are not. So go to that place. Look at things differently and you may see them that way.

....

■ **For many of us, our past is like a police car in our rearview mirror.** We expect it to stop us at any moment.

....

■ **The status quo is quaking.** The system is rebooting. Stability doesn't live here any more. Mobility is mandatory. Get going because the going is as good as it is going to get.

....

■ **It's not about hierarchy, it's about heterarchy**—where leaders and followers are interchangeable depending on circumstances. The matrix is the message. Everyone has a license to create a better way. Influence is earned daily. Authority is by invitation only. Informal power and formal structures overlap. Titles are inevitable, and they're even respected but they're merely a credential. So are you managing by title? Or are you leading by example?

....

MY MANTRAS

_____

_____

_____

_____

_____

_____

_____

_____

■ **The Generational Divide may be smaller than you think.** Boomers and Gen-Xers are already close. But Boomers and Gen-Yers can get even closer. There is a middle path where they can meet to create remarkable results. The best Boomers have the wisdom to meet Gen-Yers more than halfway. With more than half the workforce over 40, Boomers still have the power but they're learning a new game that's being defined by the Gen-Yers.

■ **Experience can be a liability if it's rooted in obsolete realities.** The most successful organizations are characterized by a mutual admiration for each other. Mentoring flows both ways. Age has its advantages but youth has technology.

■ **Master the rules.** In a post-excess reality, every category is being constrained by terms of compliance that can verge on insanity. It's as much about doing things right as it is about doing the right things. The pendulum has swung to the extreme and it may be a while before it swings back. So don't complain, comply.

■ **The champions treat compliance like gravity.** It is what it is. They operate within it. They're creative in the space open to them. They don't allow the "administrivia" to excuse them for not excelling. The process is not the enemy but one's attitude can be. Compliance can set you free to go deep on what really matters.

■ **Gravity never responds to complaints that it's unfair.** If you mess with gravity, you'll fall on your butt. What else in your life is like that?

MY MANTRAS

I ADAPT BY:

Identify the three most effective ways that enable you to adapt to change and complexity. Explore how you can adapt even more skillfully. Find role models and study their Adaptive Navigation.

MY OPPORTUNITIES ARE:

Discern three immediate, lucrative opportunities to thrive. Repeat every week.

_____

_____

_____

_____

_____

_____

_____

_____

_____

_____

_____

_____

_____

_____

_____

_____

_____

_____

_____

_____

_____

I FOCUS ON:

Focus on the three things that will give you the highest "ROE" – Return On Energy. Dismiss as many things as possible that don' t feed your focus.

MY MANTRAS

FULL EXPRESSION

Desire to fully develop and express one's talent and personality; need to communicate authentically and spontaneously with others; determination to ensure that one's voice is heard because one believes in one's ability to make an impact; inspired performance sustained by a passion for the grind; reverse of regret and procrastination; appreciation that we're all either amplifiers or inhibitors of each other's power.

MANTRA:

"I declare my interdependence. I'm all-in and I'm playing full out."

FULL EXPRESSION

■ Every day is an entire career in miniature.

· ·

■ Be powerful not perfect.

· ·

■ **Embrace your inner superpower – your capacity to be amazing.** We all have a personal genius that that endows us with unique gifts. Our lifelong personal mission is to be worthy of them.

· ·

■ **Be yourself because others are already taken.** I have never heard anyone say, "I should never have been authentic." I often hear people say, "I wish I would have said exactly what I mean. If only I had been true to myself."

· ·

■ **Once upon a time, there was a girl in first grade who was asked by her teacher to draw anything she wanted.** She started drawing earnestly. The teacher asked her what she was drawing. She replied, "I'm drawing God." The teacher said, "But no one knows what God looks like." The girl replied, "They will in a minute."

· ·

▓ **Practice the Principle of Makoto.** Say what you're going to do, then do it. When you speak, it must be as though it is already done.

▓ **If you sit, just sit.** If you stand, just stand. But don't wobble.

▓ **What will it take for you to be Amazing?** I define "Amazing" as causing others to be delighted, thrilled, motivated, inspired, joyous, excited, or happy. When you're amazing, you restore others' faith in their future. You remind them of what's possible. You cause their rejuvenation. You become the bridge between where they are and where they can be.

MY MANTRAS

■ When the *force* is with you, you don't need force.

■ Play in the gap between what is and what's possible.

■ **Choose a side. Get in the game.** No one listens to the voices from the grandstand and no one cares about the win-loss record of the referee.

■ **No matter how many opportunities you've lost in the past, believe that you will win the next one.** And do the hard work to make it happen.

■ **"It's always your next move."**
~ *Napoleon Hill*

■ **Where can you earn the highest ROA –** *Return On Attention?* What will give you the biggest buzz? Where can you become a master of your domain? What space will open up your gifts?

MY MANTRAS

▧ **In evolutionary terms, the great innovations often come in times of drought or famine.** In tough times, there are no resources to solve the problems the old way, so new ways must be found.

▧ **Knock, knock, this is obsolescence calling.** We should all be running a little scared. We should all be reinventing ourselves in advance of the famine or drought. "Routine" may be the most dangerous word in business.

MY MANTRAS

_____

_____

_____

_____

_____

_____

_____

_____

_____

_____

_____

_____

_____

_____

_____

■ **When you have moments of magic, freeze that frame.** Ask yourself what inspired them so you can reproduce more of them, especially the ones that you've created from within.

■ **Whatever isn't adding value is being stripped away.** Bare is beautiful. Flat is the new up. The optics are as important as anything else. We all need to consistently demonstrate and communicate how essential we are.

■ **Let go of those things that don't serve you anymore.**

■ **The highest level of influence is when we inspire others to be remarkable.** We expand their capacity to create extraordinary results. We help them trust themselves to handle situations that may have previously been beyond their grasp. Who would you have to be to inspire others to be like that?

■ **If you want to cause transformation, you have to talk in a way that will make people listen.**

■ **Before you can do something, you must first be something.**

▓ **Play like your life depends on how you handle this meeting.** It does, you're building a habit.

. . . .

▓ **There is no such thing as a small win.** A win is a win. The more you win, the more you build the habit of winning. Make every win a Super Bowl victory in your own mind. Even when you don't achieve the desired result, find a way to make it a win. Your subconscious doesn't understand the difference between the actual result and your interpretation of it.

. . . .

▓ **Inform your body and your face who you are.** Look like the person you want others to believe you are.

. . . .

MY MANTRAS

_____

_____

_____

_____

_____

_____

_____

_____

_____

_____

_____

▨ **There are moments we need to move, and there are moments we need to be still.** Stillness without action is stagnation. But action without stillness is burnout.

▨ **We need to embrace our opposites.** Our strengths always have a corresponding weakness. Our greatest moments are born in our lowest moments. Wherever we gain power, we lose it somewhere else.

▨ **Here's the paradox of the human pursuit— home may be the place where we find comfort, relaxation, and belonging, but it's also the place we have to leave in order to grow, create and prosper.** So home must be mobile. It must become the place you carry within you wherever you go.

▨ **"And so much of my life has been about returning home and longing for home, wanting my children to know about my roots.** And I thought I can't be the only one to feel this way so I thought it would be an interesting topic to explore." ~ *Sela Ward*

▓ "You can't be too self-confident because there is never enough self-confidence. Courage is fear that has said its prayers. I understand that now just like I understand that theater is a great, adrenalized place to work." ~ *Diane Lane*

▓ Become living proof of what practice can make.

▓ The Evolution Manual is simple: do whatever it takes to survive, listen to your instincts, preserve yourself, stick together, procreate and protect what you procreate. It's all programmed into our DNA. But survival doesn't equal happiness. Success and happiness are conscious pursuits that must be made daily.

MY MANTRAS

_____

_____

_____

_____

_____

_____

_____

_____

_____

_____

■ **Our fiercest competitors are our truest partners.** They're educating customers, expanding markets and making us better.

■ **Mastery isn't the same as graduation.** No-one rings a bell and declares you a guru or a master to anyone. It's earned over decades. It stands the test of time, adversity, and change.

■ **People are at their best when they're most interested in what's going on around them.** In those situations, it's easier to focus because the distractions are much weaker.

■ **When we are bored, we're vulnerable to anything that offers us an escape from our apathy.** By developing an intense interest in subjects that stretch and test our limits, we immunize ourselves against the sideways drift or the downward creep.

■ **Just because your eyes are open, it doesn't mean that you're awake.**

■ **There is a direct correlation between interest and optimism.** One cannot be indifferent and upbeat at the same time.

Confidence in the future is married to passion for the present.

"I believe that magic is real. I believe fantasy is real. I live halfway between reality and fantasy all the time." ~ *Lady Gaga*

Winning doesn't mean someone else loses. It means expanding the possibilities for all your stakeholders. That's the power of exponential versus incremental thinking. One beautifully executed idea can change your world so stretch for it.

MY MANTRAS

_____

_____

_____

_____

_____

_____

_____

_____

_____

_____

_____

_____

_____

■ **In cataclysmic times, playing small doesn't count.** Big storms demand big plays.

....

■ **Get out of your own way.** Be conscious of yourself but don't be self-conscious. Great actors don't allow their nerves to interfere with their performance. They use them to amplify their performance. They remember it's always about the audience. Or, in the case of a salesperson, the customer. Right now I'm concentrating all my energy on a single goal: making these few words extremely rewarding for you. What are you concentrating on?

....

■ **Package yourself across channels.** Start somewhere. Begin by being spectacular on the phone and in-person (e-mail doesn't count). Set up your Facebook page. Spice up your LinkedIn profile. Create a personal website. Experiment with video and podcasts – we're all being trained to absorb our key data this way. Get the right people to help you. There are thousands of good people out there who are both skilled and inexpensive.

....

■ **Make your charisma a core discipline.**
Charisma is the ability to influence others in
an uplifting way. Charisma is also hard work.
It's a learned skill that draws on our natural
gifts. It's fuelled by mastery. It's not about
overstatement and self promotion. It's about
contribution and value to others.

■ **Some of the most magnetic people I know
are also the most understated.** But they're
always on and they always bring their A-game.

■ **Reap the "Inspiration Dividend."** Customers
want something extraordinary and they're
willing to pay for it.

MY MANTRAS

_____

_____

_____

_____

_____

_____

_____

_____

_____

_____

_____

▨ **Be a YES waiting to happen even when you hear NO.** NO doesn't mean never. It just means not now.

▨ **Rediscover your genius.** It's the one thing you do so well that others are amazed by it. In case you haven't noticed, mine is talking and writing. What's yours?

▨ **There's no magic bullet, just a magical journey.** Abracadabra. It's time to be magical, so go cast your spell.

■ **Be a Maestro.** Maestro is the Italian word for master or teacher. It comes from the world of classical music, but it is also the ultimate professional accolade. Maestro is the title awarded to people who inspire us through their mastery of their art. It may be the art of music, painting, theatre, dancing, cooking, manufacturing, design, business, presentations, consulting, sales, service or just living. But it's the execution of those disciplines at a level that strikes us as art. Develop your knowledge and skills to such a level that it occurs to others as an art form. To quote the great Tina Turner, be "Simply The Best."

MY MANTRAS

■ **Amateurs wait for inspiration.** Professionals just get down to work.

■ **"What players want is to feel they can play well: not told what to do, but offered possibilities."** ~ *Colin Davis, conductor*

■ **Live the perception that you want others to have of you.** Do the work that needs to be done. Until others relate to you as someone of value, you will be trying to express a message inconsistent with what you represent. That's why I have created this book. It's another deposit on the franchise that I'm building with my community of Stars.

■ **Competence At the Level of a Maestro, (CALM) means you have the required knowledge and skill to perform at the highest level.** It means you can carry the expectations and weight the tasks demand. CALM is the quality that takes people's breath away. It's the element that elicits the surprise and wonder that captivates others. It's the behaviour that begs the question, "how does she do that?"

■ **There is no short cut to Competence At the Level of Maestro.** While the process can be accelerated, it's always going to be a long journey because it has no end point. The pursuit of CALM is a state of never-ending personal enhancement for its own sake. Sometimes it's a pleasure and sometimes it's blood, sweat and tears; but it's always a passion that grows more intense over time.

■ **CALM is the signal that cuts through the noise and doubt.** It's the one measurable success factor that can be seen, heard, felt, tasted and touched, but never faked. It's where the rubber meets the road. And the more sophisticated the audience or participants, the greater the impact.

■ **CALM means rising beyond being a "True Pro" to being someone whose expertise is creating a new level of performance.**

MY MANTRAS

■ Your personal expression is governed by the space you earn in the minds of the people around you.

■ Enrich your vocabulary. If you don't have a word for it, you don't miss it and you can't get it. If you cannot describe it, you cannot create it. Words are packages of possibility. Develop a vocabulary that gives you access to a new future.

■ As you become more powerful with language you see more possibilities and you make more possibilities happen.

▨ Speak as though this is the last five minutes you're ever going to have here.

....

▨ **Be memorable.** Unleash your inner entertainer. Say it loud or say it soft, but say it. Make others' day by making an impact. Make yourself bigger by playing a bigger role in the lives of your constituents. Choose your moments and take them.

....

▨ Get out there and meet somebody. Campaigns are never won from the comfort of your office. Pick up the phone. Attend the meetings. Join the associations. Press the flesh. Look people in the eye and make a connection. And yes, blog, Tweet, Facebook, and get LinkedIn.

....

MY MANTRAS

_____

_____

_____

_____

_____

_____

_____

_____

_____

_____

■ **Don't just download, upload.** Create your own podcasts and videos. It's never been easier to broadcast your message to the world.

. . . .

■ **It's one thing to maximize your value; it's another to communicate it fabulously.** The winners understand perception is reality. They know they're defined by their words and actions. They're conscious of themselves but they're not self-conscious. They understand how to differentiate themselves not just through the value they deliver, but how they make others feel while they deliver it.

. . . .

■ **Function and feeling are intertwined.** Show them the money, but show them the love as well. So what's your story? What is your magnetic promise? What sets you apart from everyone else in your space? Why would the best customers want to buy from you? And why would the best performers want to partner with you?

. . . .

MY MANTRAS

_____

_____

_____

_____

_____

■ **Dramatic Differentiation is the game-changer.** It's what sets you apart so others want part of you. We're all in competition for the same thing: other people's time. We're lucky if we get our 15 minutes. We have to earn it through dramatic personal differentiation. Then we have to earn the next 15 minutes and the next. In fact, our entire future depends on the caliber of 15-minute increments we can keep earning.

■ **Dramatic Differentiation can be in the flick of a wrist, the turn of a phrase or the wink of an eye.** It's the Law of Disproportionate Reward. The smallest distinction, the babiest action, the slightest touch, the skimpiest move can make a massive impact that ripples through our future.

MY MANTRAS

_____

_____

_____

_____

_____

_____

_____

_____

_____

■ **Imagine a $100 bill floating by.** You would just reach and grab it. You wouldn't think about whether you look good while you're grabbing it. You would just do it. What else do you need to just do?

■ **Are you a player or a spectator?** What has being a spectator cost you?

■ **The point is not to do it right.** It's to do it right now.

MY UNIQUE TALENT IS:

Define your unique talent clearly and convincingly. Express it in a way that inspires you to develop it. Share it with others who you trust. Get their feedback. Keep refining it until you believe it's true.

MY POWERFUL MESSAGE IS:

Choose the powerful message that you stand for. Think about the best way for you to communicate it. Practice it. Inspire yourself.

I AMPLIFY OTHERS' POWER BY:

Think about how you can amplify others'
power. Develop your capacity for making others
successful. Identify role models around you and
learn from them.

EMOTIONAL CONTROL

Ability to choose one's emotions constructively in the face of chaos, crisis or uncertainty; capacity to control one's feelings through logic and reasoning in extreme circumstances; presence of mind to take the right actions in the eye of the storm; achieved through mindful practice and self-evaluation; mental sharpness to see what's pivotal in dire situations and the emotional toughness to act accordingly.

MANTRA

"No one and no thing can make me do what shouldn't be done. I choose my response. I own my actions."

EMOTIONAL CONTROL

■ **Happiness is having no regrets.**

....

■ **Shake hands with your shadow.** The bigger you become, the bigger your challenges become. Doubt is just another word for human. Fear is just another word for respect. Courage requires both qualities.

....

■ **Our actions cause our feelings, which cause more actions.** It's a virtuous circle. We own our moods. We need to act our way into feeling great, rather than feeling our way into acting great.

....

■ **Complaining is never a source of power.** How you react today determines others' response to you tomorrow.

....

■ **We become what we complain about.**

....

MY MANTRAS

_____

_____

_____

_____

_____

■ **To everyone else, the only thing that matters is our actions.** Everything else, is an internal matter. No one else can see or hear what's going on inside our minds. The quality of our relationships with others is a direct function of the quality of our actions.

••

■ **Before we build great relationships with others, we need to build great relationships with ourselves.** We need to see the person in the mirror as our ultimate champion.

••

■ **Be consciously fascinated.** Consider the possibilities. Don't automatically agree but don't automatically disagree. Ask yourself the question, "What happens if they're right?" Let the insights in. Allow them to frolic in your brain. Who knows what magic they can create there?

••

■ **Whatever you take for granted gets taken away.** Focus on the magic, not the tragic.

••

■ **Emotions are generated by historical associations.** Certain patterns are hardwired into us culturally, genetically and individually. The more tuned in we are to our emotions, the more consciousness we can bring to our decisions. And the greater our control over them.

••

■ "In the complex interplay of slower, conscious reason and quicker, subconscious emotion, the basic architecture of the brain ensures that we feel first and think second. Then, in our ongoing response to potential peril, the way the brain is built and operates assures that we are likely to feel more and think less." ~ *Joseph LeDoux, Neuroscientist, New York University*

••

■ Emotions can be entirely realistic. Sometimes running away is the most courageous option. The best fight is the one you don't have.

••

■ How much time do you spend being upset and angry? How well is that working out for you? Being self-righteous makes others wrong and that never turns out well. Do you want to be right or do you want to be happy?

••

■ "It's more important to know what kind of person has a disease than what kind of disease a person has." ~ *Norman Cousins*

••

■ Every thought creates an emotion and every emotion creates an associated chemical reaction. Think healthy. Feel healthy. Be healthy.

••

■ Whoever you are making wrong is making you angry.

....

■ When you're angry with someone, you allow them to live rent free in your head. They may not even know you exist. Evict them now and invite someone beautiful to stay.

....

■ Even monkeys fall out of trees. Forgive yourself.

....

■ You cannot shake hands with a closed fist. Let go of your anger so you can open yourself up to others.

....

■ One cannot hold onto anything if one grips too tightly.

....

■ Of all the things you could be, why would you be mean?

....

MY MANTRAS

_____

_____

_____

_____

_____

_____

_____

_____

■ **Reason without emotion doesn't work.**
Without recognizing our body's reactions, we
have no guide to what decision will be best for
us. There's far too much information to make
a completely rational decision anyway. Think
about it: we do a Google search that gets mil-
lions of hits and we only look at the first page
because that's all we have time for.

. . . .

■ **"Let's all be rational here" is never an appro-
priate thing to say because it's impossible.**

. . . .

■ **Things may not be what we think.** The
meaning of things comes from their "emotional tagging." An emotional tag is the way we file
things in our brain and body. It's the feeling
we experienced when we first encountered
them or something similar. We feel things first,
then we think, talk or act accordingly.

. . . .

■ **Motion is driven by emotion.** Facts are
informed by feeling. Decisions are determined
by heart and mind in equal measure.

. . . .

MY MANTRAS

_____

_____

_____

_____

■ **Most people struggle to express the core trends defining their future.** They find it hard because they're trying to describe their rational response to the question. If they were asked to describe their emotions, they would find it easier. Work back from the emotion to identify what's causing the emotion.

....

■ **Much of our behaviour is self-medication.** We're always trying to rectify our poor emotional states and reestablish equilibrium. We're trying to move from fear of uncertainty to control of our destiny.

....

MY MANTRAS

■ The impulse to act is emotional, the decision whether to act is rational.

....

■ We all go through moments of scarcity in pursuit of moments of abundance. How we manage ourselves in those moments determines what happens next. Remember: other people don't know that we're being uncharacteristically desperate or anxious. They think that's simply who we are. One phone call or one meeting can colour other people's perception of us forever.

....

■ Life is a grindstone – it can wear us down or sharpen us up. It's our choice.

....

■ "Nothing is enough for the person to whom enough is too little." ~ *Epicurus*

....

■ Run your own MCTV – mental circuit television. Observe yourself interacting with others. Ask yourself, "If I were them, would I want to be with me?"

....

■ Intense emotions are intoxicating. Literally. They can exhilarate, energize and enthuse us to great heights. Or they can paralyze, poison or plunge us into great despair.

....

■ When the fire dies down, the predators come in.

....

■ While you're running from something, make sure you're running to something.

....

■ Excitement generates adrenaline that electrifies us into action. It is short lived. That's why we need to keep generating it in ourselves and others.

....

MY MANTRAS

■ Inside every hurt and setback is a learning of equal or greater power. We lose things as we grow older. It's only by embracing one's losses that one can gain from them.

••

■ Multiple times an hour, we confront temptations to be depressed, distracted or drawn to problems. We need to access "uplifters" that will pull us back on track. An uplifter is any thought that energizes or excites us into powerful actions.

••

■ "On the basis of the latest brain research, as well as practical experience, let's acknowledge this profound truth: altruism and generosity can be hedonistic pleasures."
~ *Nicholas Kristof*

••

■ **I am in continual pitch mode.** In any given week, I initiate or respond to twenty opportunities to deliver a motivational program to clients. I only succeed with two to three opportunities. That means I spend 85-90 percent of my time dealing with disappointment. My success is a direct function of my ability to endure failure. After all these years, I always expect to win. It always hurts to lose. The secret is to get over it quickly. It's asymmetrical. Every win immediately erases the preceding losses.

■ **Here is Lipkin's recipe for failure: try to please everybody.** There will always be people who don't buy you. Don't sell yourself short because you can't sell them on you. Focus your will on the willing.

■ **One sentence from you can become a life sentence for someone else.**

■ **Don't try to make your children happy.** Make them responsible for their own happiness.

MY MANTRAS

_____

_____

_____

_____

■ **Beware of your negatives because negatives are three times more powerful than positives.** People are far more vocal about their negative emotions than they are about their positive ones. If up to 5% of people are unhappy with you, that's acceptable. Even 10% is workable. At 15%, you're in a marginal situation. At 20%, the odds have swung against you.

••

■ **Remind yourself why you're gifted.** You're blessed with an abundance of assets. Take stock both inside and out. Gratitude is a source of great power.

••

■ **The little things are not small at all.** When they're gone, you'll realize how epic they really were.

••

■ **"I never saw a wild thing sorry for itself.** A small bird will drop frozen dead from a bough without ever having felt sorry for itself."
~ *D. H. Lawrence*

••

MY MANTRAS

_____

_____

_____

_____

_____

■ **A cheetah misses its prey nine out of ten times.** Yet it hunts until it eats. Giving up is not an option for the cheetah and it's not an option for you. Celebrate your misses – they're proof that you're still in the hunt. And every hunt makes you stronger, faster, better.

· ·

■ **Life is too serious to be taken too seriously, especially if people's lives are not at stake.** Self-righteousness and happiness are incompatible. Our biggest source of amusement should be ourselves. Laughing at yourself may be the best way to get others to laugh with you.

· ·

MY MANTRAS

■ **Smiling is the most attractive way to arrange your face.** It's also the easiest way to instantly feel good. Smile and laugh easily and you'll find a whole lot of people wanting to share your humour with you.

••

■ **You have more smiles in you than you use.** But whatever smiles you don't use, you lose. The smile and the moment go together. Make the most of both of them.

••

■ **The more fun you have, the more funds you'll make.** Pursue happiness in pursuit of revenue.

••

MY EMOTIONS OF CHOICE:

Choose the five emotions that you want to experience most often. Seize every opportunity to feel them. Explore how you can even use difficult situations to feel these emotions.

MY POWERFUL ACTIONS:

Identify your most powerful actions in crisis moments. Use the next crisis to act. Make it a habit.

MY "MINDFUL" SITUATIONS:

Determine the situations where you are not at your best. Think about the circumstances that cause you discomfort. Be mindful of them and deliberately control your emotions in those moments.

Focus on diet, exercise and self-transformation to create a healthy life; determination to shape one's body and mind with all the tools available; direct function of one's love of life and desire to preserve it as long as possible; prioritizing one's total wellbeing over everything else; appreciation of the ecosystem that we all form with each other.

MANTRA

"Age is my friend. I am an athlete. I can be sharper, smarter, stronger every day."

COMMITMENT TO HEALTH

■ **Today's most prevalent emotion is chronic fatigue.** It's taking all we have just to stay where we are. So much is coming at us so fast, it's hard to know what to focus on, never mind what to do about it. We're exhausted and we're in desperate need of more energy. We're tired of being tired. We want to feel alive and excited.

■ **Age is no longer an indication of youth.** 60 is the new 30. From rock stars to thought leaders, seniors are sizzling. Boomers are regenerating themselves and their role in the future. They're rediscovering their mojo. They're bridging the generational divide. The new winners are hungry for *kaizen* – constant and never-ending improvement.

■ **Be serious about having fun and have fun when you're being serious.**

MY MANTRAS

The ratio of positive to negative factors in our life determines our overall health. It's like cholesterol. Cholesterol is composed of HDL, high density lipids, and LDL, low density lipids. The HDL are like the positive factors and the LDL are like the negative factors. The ratio of one to the other determines our overall health or happiness.

There are two kinds of negatives – low intensity and high intensity. The low intensity negatives include feelings of disappointment, fatigue, pessimism, apathy, unappreciation, and discomfort. The high intensity negatives include stress, alarm, anger, pain, bitterness and hate.

Low intensity negatives can turn us into victims. This is where we complain about the status quo but we don't take action. The situation may be chronic in the sense that we've become used to it. The negativity becomes habitual and we become has-beens.

MY MANTRAS

■ **High intensity negatives galvanize us into action.** We perceive them as a clear and present danger. They occur to us like armed intruders or wild marauders. So we respond instantly. We boil the frog quickly.

■ **If we want to move people into action, we need to transform their low intensity negatives into motivating forces.** We need to heighten the intensity through urgency and imagination. For example, if someone is being apathetic, we need to find the trigger that ignites their passion. If they're angry, we need to find a way to tap into their inner calm.

■ **In life, it's usually the high intensity negatives that are addressed.** The majority of people will only take action when they believe things are broken. Don't wait for them to break. Enhance them before you need to repair them.

■ **We're drowning in deadlines, but we long for lifelines.** The higher the pressure, the greater the need for a release valve. It may be another person or another experience. Either way, if we want to stay alive, every exhausting deadline must be matched by an empowering lifeline. The alternative is to be a dead person walking or dead.

■ **The stuff of sagas, fables, legends and myths is the journey through hell to get to bliss.** We can't experience bliss without going through our own hell. So the next time you find yourself going through hell, see it as preparation for bliss.

MY MANTRAS

■ **We need the balance between sleep and activity.** We can't do anything in a state of exhaustion. Constant movement is merely manic. Being still is the precursor to progress.

. . . .

■ **We're all part of each other's emotional fields.** Whatever you're feeling, others in your orbit will feel too.

. . . .

■ **Health isn't only correlated with positive emotions.** Health is comprised of opposites – happiness, excitement, confidence, disappointment, fatigue, confusion, and pain. It takes one kind of emotion to illuminate its opposite.

. . . .

Power is about flow. You can't experience one extreme without experiencing its polar opposite. A vacation without work to go back to is hell. It loses its reason for being.

All play and no work will diminish our productive capacity. All work and no play will burn us out. Relaxation and stress go together like white on rice.

Every day is an opportunity to begin all over again. So measure your results, monitor your evolution, encourage feedback and listen intensely. Learning is oxygen for the mind so breathe easy.

Your attitude towards exercise defines your capacity for exercise. Emotional stress can affect blood flow and metabolism. Tension makes our breaths short and shallow. We absorb less oxygen which makes us feel even more tense and the constrictive cycle continues. Change your mind, change your actions, change your body, change your life.

MY MANTRAS

■ **Take a stand.** Don't sit still. The chair is not your friend. Move around. Walk more. Every time you move your muscles, you combat inertia. Every action counts. Stretch, extend, shift, reach.

■ **Negative words tend to have a bigger impact than positive ones.** We are more disturbed by someone saying, "I'm angry with you because you cheated me," than we are inspired by someone saying, "I'm pleased with you because your work was excellent."

■ **Simply by changing our language, we can change our lives.** We live inside the way we describe our lives. If we open up our vocabulary, we open up our world.

■ **Too much of a good thing is not always a good thing.** Hunger can be a great motivator, gluttony never is. Appetite is a great servant but a shocking master.

■ **The four most dangerous words in the English language are, "All You Can Eat."** If you want to live longer, eat less.

▨ **Success is a numbers game.** The more we do, the more mistakes we make, the more we adapt, and the more we win. Life rewards us for action. It also tests us with failure, rejection, and disappointment. It will wear us down or sharpen us up.

▨ **The greater our stamina and resilience, the greater our ability to endure and triumph.** Take care of yourself so you can take never-ending action.

▨ **Resilience and idealism are each other's bodyguards.**

MY MANTRAS

■ **Relish the moment and replenish your Mojo.** A relaxed mind is a resourceful mind. Think about the people, places, things, food, experiences, and feelings that give you joy. Then spread it.

■ **Burn bright but don't burn out.** Above all, take care of yourself. Pay yourself first. Recharge between sets so you can reset yourself. Take timeouts so you can be outstanding.

■ **Everything has its season.** And every season has a beginning, middle and end. But every season renews itself year after year. Just like you. This too shall pass so make it magnificent.

Life is a long walk. Sometimes, we may need to lie low and sometimes, we need to blaze our own trail.

"He who limps is still walking."
~ *Stanislaw Lec*

It is better to take imperfect steps than none at all. Get out there and do something.

Age and youth are states of mind and body. Some of the most energized people I know are well north of 70. Longevity is about the years you put into your life. Happiness is about the life you put into your years.

MY MANTRAS

■ **"Even I don't wake up looking like Cindy Crawford."** ~ *Cindy Crawford* Looking good is hard work. We all need to make ourselves up. Our daily challenge is to make the most of our natural gifts, inside and out.

■ **Everybody loves to win but only a few love to train.** Less than one out of five people have a regimented training plan – mental and physical. It's not about time-management. It's about priority management.

■ **Health and fitness come from doing what we don't feel like doing when we don't feel like doing it.** But we always feel fabulous afterwards.

■ **What matters most should receive the most time.** The winners find the time for what counts. They expand their capacity to be remarkable so they achieve more without doing more. So how are you training to win? What's your plan? And how disciplined are you in executing it?

MY MANTRAS

_____

_____

_____

■ **Winning is not about who is right; it's about who is left.** It's about falling down seven times, standing up eight. It's about the size of one's heart and lungs. It's about playing like your life depends on it, even though it doesn't, although the quality of your life ultimately does.

■ **The future belongs to those who are conditioned to win.** They take care of themselves first because they know everything else depends on it. They treat themselves like the athlete every human must be. They have a plan that's just right for them. They know that they're different – just like everybody else. They love to triumph and they love to train. One doesn't happen without the other.

MY MANTRAS

125

■ **The velocity of change is doing violence to our sense of well being.** It's exciting and exhausting in equal measure. Whatever it takes out of us, we have to put back in, and then some.

■ **We're all living in the confluence of a perfect storm.** There is more to do, and less time to do it. There are so many other people who can do it well and so many people depending on us to get it right. Anxiety, overwhelm and fatigue are the new normal. No matter how much the economy improves, uncertainty is the new certainty.

Our happiness is a direct function of our capacity to handle anxiety, overwhelm and fatigue. It's mental, emotional, physical and social. It's the stamina we show in life's over-time moments. It's in the crises that we define who we are and what others become.

Love the life that you have, no matter what. Live life powerfully no matter what circumstances it throws at you.

Achieve "the kind of happiness that doesn't depend on what happens." ~ *David Steindl-Rast*

Understand the source of your results and focus on feeding it. Take care of the roots if you want to enjoy the fruits.

MY MANTRAS

I CREATE A HEALTHY LIFE BY:

Identify the three most impactful ways for you to create a healthy life. Commit to them by starting today. Recommit every morning.

I LOVE MY LIFE BECAUSE:

*Remind yourself why you love your life and
what you love most about it. Then live your life
in a way that honours your love.*

_____

_____

_____

_____

_____

_____

_____

_____

_____

_____

_____

_____

_____

_____

_____

_____

_____

_____

_____

_____

_____

_____

I CONTRIBUTE TO MY
ECOSYSTEM THROUGH:

Think about how your health contributes to the health of the people around you. Remember how important your health is to theirs.

MY MANTRAS

UNCOMMON PURPOSE

Awareness of a higher intelligence and an intense desire to understand how it impacts one's life; search for a higher purpose that gives meaning to one's day-to-day activities; superior ability to cope with adversity through empowering interpretation; a rich inner life; service to one's fellow human beings.

MANTRA

"I am in touch with my inner superhero. I will play big because I am part of something bigger than me."

UNCOMMON PURPOSE

■ **The clearer, the briefer, the better.**

....

■ **Simple doesn't mean easy.** It just means it's easily understood.

....

■ **The problem with life is that it's so daily.** The real question is not whether you'll play at your best every day. Like Tim Hortons, you need to be "Always Fresh." It's how you're going to use your best every day to make others even better.

....

■ **No matter how old you are right now, you are growing older right now.** That's automatic. Growing wiser is intentional. Becoming valuable happens on purpose.

....

■ **We cannot change our DNA, but we can change our direction.** A tiny shift can open up a whole new view. If there is one thing I've learnt from studying over a million people, it's that we can consciously choose what to pay attention to. Then we can decide to take action. We can sustain our focus. We can develop new habits. And then we can help others do the same.

....

■ **Great happiness doesn't come from great events, it comes from great appreciation of small events.** By definition, great events are few and far between. Births, graduations, weddings, promotions, start-ups, inventions, big deals and round-the-world trips may not be everyday events. But it's the everyday events that ultimately determine the quality of our everyday lives.

....

■ **Happiness is a function of our ability to derive maximum pleasure from the things we do most often.**

....

■ **Your happiness is not just your happiness, it determines the happiness of everyone who encounters you.** If you motivate others when you speak to them, you're a motivational speaker. If not, they will vote with their legs and walk away.

....

MY MANTRAS

■ **Happiness can be stored and accessed at will.** It can be as simple as a fresh orange or a firm banana. It can be a warm jacket in winter or comfortable shoes on a long walk. We've all stored good feelings in things and people around us. They're magical. We need to recognize what they are and who they are. Then we need to get close to them.

··

■ **Become a "talisman" for others.** A talisman is anything that exercises a powerful influence on human feelings or emotions. In all our interactions with others, we want to be "tagged" as a magical presence in others' lives.

··

■ **Hierarchy doesn't cut it anymore.** The further away one moves from the frontline, the less relevant one becomes. Position doesn't equal power. Power is earned by invitation only. It's about cooperation, not manipulation. Life is too transparent to be selfish.

··

■ **Simplicity sells.** Whatever cuts through the cacophony sticks in your mind.

··

■ **Mastery is a conscious competence that is amplified by a desire and ability to share it.**

··

■ At some point, there is always going to be a gap between what you know and what you have to know – the past versus the future. If you have prepared all you can to win and you take the leap, it will work out the way you planned. Or it will work out in a way that was unimaginable at the starting line. In either case, it always works out.

· ·

■ The past and present is in the future. And the future is in the past and present.

· ·

■ There is an ancient African saying that states, "A person is a person because of other people." Our worth is measured by the value we bring to those around us.

· ·

MY MANTRAS

_____

_____

_____

_____

_____

_____

_____

_____

_____

_____

_____

_____

■ **To earn others' interest, we need to represent their interests.** Other people must be enrolled in our offering because it resonates so strongly with them. Ultimately, there are only two kinds of people – the people we have to be with and the people we want to be with.

■ **How do people feel about themselves after a meeting with you?** Do they feel bigger, faster, or stronger? Do you liberate their superpower? Do you encourage them to dare? Do they feel like they can take more on? Are you a tailwind or a headwind?

■ **Some of the most inspirational people are understated and introverted.** They set an example that inspires others. Others are bold and intrepid. Heroes come in all shapes and sizes.

....

■ **A hero is someone who is regarded as a model or ideal to others because of her actions.** They are proof it can be done.

....

■ **There is a direct correlation between inspiration and the size of the problem.** The greater the problem, the greater the inspiration required to solve it.

....

MY MANTRAS

_____

_____

_____

_____

_____

_____

_____

_____

_____

_____

_____

_____

_____

■ Be a celebrator: someone who habitually proclaims their appreciation; someone who praises others widely and champions their success; someone who commemorates the moment with a party, a ceremony and an uninhibited good time.

■ **Share everything.** Be generous to the point that others consider unwise. Trust everyone within your communities to do the right thing with their gifts. The more open you are, the more you open new networks and opportunities.

■ "People who are selfish have little problems but they seem big. People who are generous have big problems but they seem little."
~ *Mother Teresa*

■ **Seize the new media to broadcast yourself to the planet.** Live the mantra, "One action can become a movement."

....

■ **"If you do something, video it.** If you video something, post it. If you post something promote it to your friends. Projects shared online become inspiration for others and opportunities for collaboration. Individual makers globally connected this way become a movement. Ideas that are shared turn into bigger ideas. Projects once shared become group projects and bigger than any one person would attempt alone. And those projects can become the seeds of products and even industries. The simple act of 'making it in public' can become the engine of innovation, even if that was not the intent. It is simply what ideas do: spread when shared." ~ *Chris Anderson, Editor, Wired magazine*

....

MY MANTRAS

_____

_____

_____

_____

_____

_____

_____

■ **The new kind of leader doesn't want control. He doesn't want power.** He isn't in it for the adulation or personal deification. He's in it for the exhilaration of redefining what's possible. He wants to create extraordinary things with extraordinary people in extraordinary ways. He may be charismatic, gregarious, outgoing, effusive and vocal. Or he may be reticent, understated, and introverted. If they're backed by content and character, both styles can be equally powerful.

···

■ **Stand guard at the gate of your mind.** Catch yourself drifting. Think about who you need to be and what you need to do. Keep it front and centre. Make it a priority before it becomes a penalty. Anticipate the ecstasy of action and the agony of remorse. Intensify both emotions. Dramatize the pleasure of fulfillment, magnify the pain of wimping out.

···

■ **The saddest word in the English language is, "almost."** The two saddest words are, "It's hopeless." The three saddest words are, "I give up." The four saddest words are, "It's all your fault." The five saddest words are, "I wish this wasn't happening." The six saddest words are, "I don't want to get involved." The seven saddest words are, "I have no time for myself anymore." The eight saddest words are, "Things aren't the way they used to be." The nine saddest words are, "I can't count on anyone to get it done." The ten saddest words are, "One day they will find out I'm not good enough." Never use those words.

∙∙

■ **Tell yourself whatever story motivates you into action.** My story is that keeping you on-purpose is my reason for being. If I don't do that, I have no reason to be here. And that's about as painful as it gets for me. On the other hand, just one call from you will make it all worthwhile. What drives your engine?

∙∙

MY MANTRAS

■ **The unexpected consequences of every action will always outnumber the expected.** But if we're acting on purpose, nothing happens by accident. We make sense of things that don't appear to make sense to others.

....

■ **A man who chases two chickens catches neither.**

....

■ **Choose the character you want to be.** Success is about reinventing yourself for the part that fits best. Your customers are buying the role you can play in their lives. I am your performance enhancer. I expand your perspective and motivate you to explore options that may not have been on your radar before. My character fits this character. And every message enables me to stretch my range. What part fits you best? How meaningful is it to your customers? How are you growing into it? How are you stretching yourself?

....

MY MANTRAS
_____
_____
_____
_____
_____
_____

■ What cause are you championing? And who is championing your cause? How great is your will to win? How prepared are you to knock on doors until they open?

....

■ Take your knocks and keep on knocking.

....

■ Make a difference in something that makes a difference

....

■ When everything else is commoditized, inspiration can be the ultimate game-changer. So how inspired are you? Are you just laying rocks? Or are you creating a cathedral?

....

■ It doesn't matter whether you're naturally outgoing or not. What matters is how much you matter to as many people as possible. So whom have you helped today? And how many more can you help?

....

■ Unless you are intentional with people, you won't be present and you won't make a difference. Many people engage in small talk permanently. You don't create powerful conversations by default.

....

■ **In every difficult conversation that doesn't turn out well, who is the one person who is always there?** You.

....

■ **"Locks are on doors to keep honest people honest.** One percent of people will be honest and never steal. Another one percent will always be dishonest and try to pick your lock and steal your TV. Locks won't do much to protect you from hardened thieves. The purpose of locks is to protect you from the 98% of mostly honest people who might be tempted to try your door if it had no lock."
~ *Dan Ariely*

....

I'M HERE TO:

Discern what you are here to do. Define the biggest contribution you make to others. Declare it. Keep making it. Then keep making it bigger.

ADVERSITY MEANS:

Think about the three most difficult situations you have faced in the past month. Think about how they developed your character and your capacity. Think about why you should be grateful for the experience. Repeat every month.

I SERVE BY:

Determine the most effective ways you serve others. Think about how rewarding it is for you. Find ways to serve more people more often.

SOCIAL INTIMACY

Desire to feel part of groups where people are close to each other; need to build warm, deep friendships with others; drive to share personal insights with others that one can trust and rely on; source of validation and assurance in times of change and instability; a space to regroup and reflect on one's thoughts through the perspective of one's confidantes; as vital to one's wellbeing as anything that one does with one's body.

MANTRA

"I can face the world because of the people who've got my back. I am the company I keep."

SOCIAL INTIMACY

■ **There is no being without another being to be with.**

....

■ **The people around you are being who you are being.**

....

■ **Every meeting is an investment or withdrawal of social capital.** The wealthiest people are the people with whom others want to spend the most time.

....

■ **Having the life you want is not about just getting what you want.** It's about getting others the life they want.

....

■ **Are you participating so the people around you win?**

....

■ **See others as bigger than they see themselves, then help them grow.**

....

■ **People see themselves in you – the good, the bad and the ugly.** Be inspired so they see the inspiration that motivates them to be more, see more, do more.

....

■ **"Faster – that is, more intuitive – decisions are associated with higher levels of cooperation.** Whereas slower – that is, more reflective – decisions are associated with higher levels of selfishness. These results suggest that our first impulse is to cooperate." ~ *Adrian Ward, Scientific American, November 2012*

....

■ **Human beings are gregarious.** They not only need to be with others, they derive pleasure from doing so. Talking is how we connect with others. Language is the oxytocin that binds us together.

....

■ **We're past the point in history where an individual alone can understand what's going on.** An individual has to group with other individuals to access different perspectives. Many minds make ideas work.

....

■ **People who spend the most time talking to the most people are the most successful people.** Be the one who opens up a conversation. You may find that people are very willing to talk.

....

MY MANTRAS

_____

_____

_____

■ **"Facebook, Twitter and blogging are revolutionary tools of communication and expression.** At their best, they're changing the nature of political communication and news. But at their worst, they can become addictive substitutes for real action. How often have you heard lately, "Oh, I tweeted about that." Or "I posted that on my Facebook page." Really? In most cases that's about as impactful as firing a mortar into the Milky Way galaxy. Unless you get out of Facebook and into someone's face, you really have not acted." ~ *Thomas Friedman*

....

■ **No matter what your age, talk to young people.** They will spend more time in the future than you will. Suspend your judgments. Youth has a biological need to differentiate itself from the previous generation, just like seeds have to move away from the tree.

....

■ **People want to talk about their future.** It may be the single most important thing on their minds. They need a catalyst. They need someone with the interest and the commitment to bring it out of them. And that someone may be you.

....

■ If you ever find yourself arguing with a fool, make sure that he isn't doing the same thing.

....

■ Be an ally to all and an enemy to none.

....

■ **Like attracts like. Friendly people have friends.** Open people are surrounded by openness. Kind people generate kindness. Generous people's actions are reciprocated by others' generosity. Interested people become interesting people. What are you attracting to you?

....

■ Communicate with others like they are you and you are them.

....

■ No-one sounds like a fool in their own ears.

....

■ The essence of communication is intention. If others know that you're intensely committed to their success, they'll go through the breakdowns with you.

....

MY MANTRAS

_____

_____

_____

_____

■ **"Have I told you lately that I love you?"** ~ *Van Morrison* How many people have you told lately? How many people have told you? Feels good, doesn't it?

••

■ **The language of happiness is far more likely to be associated with social activity.** How do you feel when you hear words like togetherness, connection, conversation, party, association, sharing, support, dancing? Now think about how you feel when you hear the words alone, isolated, separated, solo, removed, aloof, detached, unaccompanied. Humans need other humans to be happy.

••

■ **You don't have to agree with others**, but they must feel as though you understand them.

••

■ **We are all a market of one.** The new champions are customizing their message, products and services to every individual customer. And we're expressing our delight or disapproval from the digital rooftops.

••

■ **Everyone matters.** Business is very, very personal. We're only as good as the way we make others feel.

••

■ "We're craving the nondigital even more these days, the authentically human interaction. We need to see some schmuck sweat."
~ *Jerry Seinfeld*

● ●

■ **Public Kudos is the ultimate currency of success.** We build our personal brands one fanatical fan at a time.

● ●

MY MANTRAS

■ Practice the Pavlovian principle – make others salivate at the thought of you because you represent such an appetizing benefit.

··

■ Practice the Labrador principle – if you always approach people with warmth and affection, eventually your warmth and affection will be rewarded.

··

■ Be courteous, kind and considerate. You never know who's watching but someone always is.

··

■ What happens in Vegas, stays on YouTube.

··

■ The hindsight of gurus and mentors provides the foresight for the next generation of gurus and mentors. Wisdom is a collaborative enterprise. Learning is a social endeavour. We're only as good as the company we keep.

··

■ Above all, do not be boring. But people who try to be too interesting are the people who become the most boring. Shine the light on others and they'll help you shine.

··

■ **Too much familiarity breeds boredom.** Too little familiarity breeds alienation. There are also two kinds of familiar – the desirable and the grudge kind. There's the familiar we love and the familiar we merely endure. What kind are you?

....

MY MANTRAS

_____

_____

_____

_____

_____

_____

_____

_____

_____

_____

_____

_____

_____

_____

_____

_____

_____

_____

■ **Human beings are naturally curious.** Our interest is "sparked" by anything that's different. We can experience interest and pleasure immediately. We can also lose it just as fast.

....

■ **We want to be around people who make us happy.** Being delightful is simply irresistible, especially when frustration or anxiety is so rampant. Embedding pleasure in every aspect of our engagement with others is a vital success skill. The more meaningful the pleasure, the longer it lasts.

....

■ **Seriousness and enjoyment are not mutually exclusive; they're each other's catalysts.**

....

■ **Live with your weaknesses but balance them with someone else's strengths.** That's the power of collaboration.

....

■ **Making others comfortable is a huge personal competitive advantage.** That means making them feel like they're in a safe place when they're in your space.

....

■ **If you want to know what someone wants, look at what they have.**

....

■ No-one ever says to someone else, "I like you because we've got big differences." Rather, we're attracted to people who we believe are just like us.

••

■ If we look for what we like in others, we're likely to see it. What's more, our focus will be reciprocated. We tend to like people who show that they like us. Admiration and affection are powerful attractors.

••

■ Be generous in the way that you listen to others.

••

■ **A Facebook friend is not really a friend.** Tweeting and texting are no substitutes for real action. A real social network is anything but virtual. "Virtual" is no substitute for virtue. The most important things in our lives are things we can touch, smell, and taste. Bricks and mortar are where we live. We are all physical beings. New and shiny is nice, but age and experience are vital. Some things can be accelerated and others take a long, long time.

....

■ **Humans are social animals.** No matter how many intermediaries are created to communicate with each other, we'll always find a way to get face to face with others. Without actual physical contact, we go insane. Loneliness is lethal. Our intelligence has evolved through our connection with each other.

....

■ **Loyalty is an emotion.** It's a belief in the benefits of a person, a company or a brand that binds us to them. It's also the holy grail of both personal and business relationships.

....

■ **The ultimate skill is the ability to build the loyalty of good people.**

....

■ A recent Bowling Green State University study found that the divorce rate for people 50-64 has doubled since 1990, and tripled for those 65 and above.

....

■ "Marriage is not a sexfest with a flawless best friend but something that takes enormous investment. There are good reasons to be romantic about marriage. The big benefit of marriage is precisely the commitment over the long term." ~ *Dr. Robert Emery, psychology professor, University of Virginia*

....

MY MANTRAS

■ **Business may not always encourage friendship, but friendship is the glue of business.** Kindness, empathy and generosity are the magic ingredients that make everything else work.

....

■ **Collaboration and cooperation don't just happen by themselves.** There is a need for rituals that bond and affiliate people with each other.

....

■ **You have no power to teach or coach until there is an affinity with your audience or team.** It's the students who give the teacher a license to share information. Acceptance precedes learning. The information cannot flow by itself.

....

■ **When we make people wrong, we close them down.**

....

■ **Communication is first and foremost about earning the right to be heard.** A community of interest must be established. People must feel connected to the subject matter and each other.

....

■ Words are like invisible bullets that we fire from a gun, or they can be like love letters that fall from the sky.

....

■ Numbers do not deal with anything that is truly important to the human spirit. Stories and examples touch us deeply and instinctively.

....

■ Leaders and teachers come to life when they tell stories that touch people's everyday lives. They make information friendlier. They invite their audiences into action because they connect at the level of heart and imagination.

....

■ When you're finished communicating, what results do you want to have achieved? Do you want people to be dead on the floor or do you want them to be inspired?

....

MY MANTRAS

_____

_____

_____

_____

_____

_____

_____

_____

■ **What's the optimal balance between being friendly and being competent?** It's the observance of the line between connection and being too familiar. It's knowing when to arrive and when to leave. It's understanding what "just enough" means. And it also means never losing one's self control emotionally or physically. Whether you're a peer or a leader, you need to get close but not too close.

· ·

■ **The key to giving people a great experience is to finish before they have had enough.** Leave them wanting more. The alternative is to go on for a minute too long and leave them irritated.

· ·

■ **At a primal level, the first question we ask ourselves when we meet someone new is: Is he dangerous?** Or, can she harm me? In scary times or in a scary place, people are far more likely to be scared. Change agents create a safe aura around themselves. They radiate reassurance.

· ·

■ **If we don't earn others' attention, we won't earn anything else from them.**

· ·

■ **Likeability is the antidote to procrastination.** People do those things they like and they postpone the rest wherever possible. They do the same with people. Likeability is also the key to sustainability. Earning others' attention and respect may win us the relationship, but affection is the glue that holds it together.

MY MANTRAS

■ **In order for people to like you, they need to believe they are like you.** They need to believe you share their values. You need to demonstrate that what's important to them is important to you.

··

■ **The greatest antidote to anxiety is community.** We can handle anything collectively. Talk is powerful. Nothing happens until someone speaks to someone else.

··

■ **No matter how old we are, a warm human voice in a trying time is the sweetest sound we can hear.** Even when we think we're just communicating the facts, we're really sharing emotions. So reach out and motivate someone. Talk directly to others. Everything else is a substitute. In the decisive moments, texting or tweeting just doesn't cut it.

··

MY MANTRAS

■ **Reach out to others.** Bring your A-game to every conversation. Be on when you need to be on. You don't need to be right, you just need to be relevant. The best ideas form themselves one dot at a time.

■ **Get out of your head and into the conversation.** If you think "I've heard all this before," you won't hear anything more. Listen like it's all new and you'll hear things you've never heard before.

■ **The other person doesn't know how often you've said the same things before.** They want to feel as though you're saying it to them for the first time. Never sound bored or monotonous no matter how many times you're repeating yourself.

MY MANTRAS

_____

_____

_____

_____

_____

_____

_____

_____

_____

■ **Friendship and leadership are inseparable.** A friend is someone who cares deeply about others, and so is a leader. A friend is someone who puts others' well-being ahead of his or her own and so is a leader. A friend is someone who others depend on and so is a leader. A friend makes it fun to be around him or her and so does a leader. A friend is someone who others choose to spend time with and so is a leader.

• •

■ **Being inspired is never a solo activity.** It's a dance between willing partners who trust each other to make the right moves. These words are mine. What are yours? Seriously, how are you going to reciprocate?

• •

■ **There's a key distinction between people tolerating us and treasuring us.** The passenger next you on the subway has little choice but to ride with you. Your colleagues may have no choice but work with you. Your partner may feel obligated for better or for worse to stay with you. Your children may simply endure you. And your mother will always love you. But what about those vital people in your life who have a choice? Are you their first choice? Are you on their Most Wanted list?

• •

■ **Are others calling you?** Do they return your calls? Are they talking about you? Do they give you preference? Do they tell you how much they value you? Do you see the smile and hear the delight in their voice when you're with them? Be a treat waiting to happen

....

■ **When people are engaged and inviting, it's intentional.** They demonstrate their appreciation for others. They put their best foot forward. They purr with pleasure. That's what makes them beautiful. It comes easier to some than others but it's always a learned skill.

....

MY MANTRAS

■ We're only as good as the people who return the promises we've kept.

....

■ Repair your connection with others by taking responsibility for things you did. Acknowledge that you were wrong. Apologize. Recreate a future that occurs to others as an opportunity for them.

....

■ "Eighty percent of the guest experience is dictated in the first ten minutes of a stay. If that doesn't go well, we've lost the guest." ~ *Ritz Carlton*

....

■ In every meeting we train people how to expect us to be in the next meeting.

....

■ Your world is shaped by your words. Make them beautiful and powerful.

....

■ Everything we do has an impact on others. We can see where it starts, but we never see where it ends.

....

I CRAVE PEOPLE WHO:

Define the people who you want to attract to you. Think about the qualities in others that you crave the most.

I BUILD MY NETWORK THROUGH:

Identify the most important ways you can build your social and professional network. Maximize your direct connection with others. Pick up the phone. Meet face to face. Earn others' time by becoming valuable to them.

I CAN BE TRUSTED TO:

Pinpoint three things that others can trust you to deliver under any circumstances.
Communicate those things to them. Then deliver. No excuses. No alibis.

GLOBAL DENIZEN

Affinity with people all over the world; strong interest in others' cultures and desire to sample their lifestyle; being a citizen of the world, not just a citizen of one's own country; a sense that anything one does can impact the world at large; an awareness that anything that happens anywhere impacts one's own life.

MANTRA

"I celebrate everyone everywhere. I am a champion of humanity."

GLOBAL DENIZEN

■ **We are all our own party.** We have our own electorate – they're our family, friends, community, customers, colleagues, and fellow-citizens of our country and our planet.

■ **How many people should be voting for you who don't even know you exist?** Why would they vote for you? Are more people voting for you today than yesterday? Or are they switching allegiances? How do you know? Simple: people vote with their legs – either toward or away from you.

■ **Besides life, liberty, the pursuit of happiness, peace, order and good government, no one owes you anything.** Even freedom from fear isn't guaranteed. Freedom isn't free. Nor is acceptance, connection, recognition, fulfillment, or prosperity. It's all earned, all the time. When we tire of campaigning, others tire of us.

■ **Depending on where you're located, it can be a very different point of view.**

■ Views are like shoes – you have to take off the old ones before you can put the new ones on. But you've invested your whole life in the old ones.

....

■ When you get rid of something, you create space for something new to arrive.

....

■ Wherever you are is where you are meant to be because that's where you are. Live there fully.

....

■ We are all immigrants in the new world. Let go of your baggage. Keep only what enables you to cross borders and boundaries.

....

■ Travel light and you'll travel a lot further.

■ "A world in which elves exist and magic works offers greater opportunities to digress and explore." ~ *Terry Brooks*

■ "We shall not cease from exploration, and the end of all our exploring will be to arrive where we started and know the place for the first time." ~ *T. S. Eliot*

■ "The Internet is becoming the town square for the global village of tomorrow." ~ *Bill Gates*

■ "I honor the place in you in which the entire universe dwells. I honor the place in you which is of love, of truth, of light, and of peace. I honor the place in you where, if you are in that place in you, and I am in that place in me, there is only one of us." ~ *Ram Dass*

■ "I learned how fast you can go from being an international hero to being a reference in a joke on a late night talk show."
~ *Michael Phelps*

■ "In any field, find the strangest thing and then explore it." ~ *John Archibald Wheeler*

■ "Creative people who can't help but explore other mental territories are at greater risk, just as someone who climbs a mountain is more at risk than someone who just walks along a village lane." ~ *R. D. Laing*

■ "It is fun to explore these kick-butt characters." ~ *Liam Neeson*

■ "You can never fully put your finger on the reason why you're suddenly, inexplicably compelled to explore one life as opposed to another." ~ *Daniel Day-Lewis*

■ "Lighting won't strike you if you stay home." ~ *Dani Reiss*

MY MANTRAS

■ "The more people explore the world, the more they realize in every country there's a different aesthetic. Beauty really is in the eye of the beholder." ~ *Helena Christensen*

■ A smile means the same thing in anyone's language.

■ I have spoken in 43 countries to over a million people. I have never met an audience that was offended because I was too enthusiastic. They love my passion for their country, their culture and the privilege of being in front of them. In every case, they appreciate my authenticity, especially because I explain why I am being like I am.

■ Celebrate your differences with others by concentrating on your commonalities. On the inside, we're all the same. The rest is there to create curiosity, stimulate dialogue, and invent new possibilities.

■ "I feel my job as an actor is to explore all sides of humanity." ~ *Kyra Sedgwick*

■ "A nation's culture resides in the hearts and in the soul of its people." ~ *Mahatma Gandhi*

■ "Culture is the process by which a person becomes all that they were created capable of being." ~ *Thomas Carlyle*

⋯⋯⋯⋯⋯⋯⋯⋯⋯⋯⋯⋯⋯⋯⋯⋯⋯⋯⋯⋯⋯

■ "Art at its most significant is a Distant Early Warning System that can always be relied on to tell the old culture what is beginning to happen to it." ~ *Marshall McLuhan*

⋯⋯⋯⋯⋯⋯⋯⋯⋯⋯⋯⋯⋯⋯⋯⋯⋯⋯⋯⋯⋯

■ "In my culture, there's a tradition that when you're in an overwhelming situation and you don't know what to do, you put yourself in a woman's shoes." ~ *Ang Lee*

⋯⋯⋯⋯⋯⋯⋯⋯⋯⋯⋯⋯⋯⋯⋯⋯⋯⋯⋯⋯⋯

■ **People are only mean when they feel threatened.** Fear breeds anger. No one is at their best when they're defending themselves against attack. Honour people's culture. Champion their cause. Be a source of reassurance and safety. And you will reap the reciprocation of their wellbeing.

■ **"Well, I think they're all basically the same story.** Every culture in the world has them. When you strip it down and analyze it, it's the young man or girl who goes through a trial or ordeal and hits a very low ebb but manages to get guidance from a Merlin type figure." ~ *Liam Neeson*

■ **"Whoever saves one life, saves the world entire."** ~ *Oscar Schindler.* We are all global microcosms. There are seven billion people in the world. Each person lives in their own world. Each world intersects in some way with every other world. Every action is a cause set in motion. If you act like the entire world hinges on your next move, you'll probably do the right thing.

MY MANTRAS

_____

_____

_____

■ **When good people do nothing, they get nothing good done.** In the game of life, there is no such thing as a bystander. We're all involved all the time. There are no timeouts.

■ **We are more influential than we think we are.** In the age of citizen journalism we all have access to global media channels. We can all make our voice heard. One conversation can help create the future. Playing small doesn't serve anyone, least of all yourself.

■ **Curiosity is an acute interest in something that appears to be unusual.** It drives the desire to discover more. It's the antidote to apathy. Curiosity and cynicism are mutually exclusive. So what are you curious about? Who are you curious about? Go find out more.

MY MANTRAS

■ "We humans quickly develop an irrational loyalty to our beliefs, and work hard to find the evidence that supports those opinions and to discredit, discount or avoid information that does not." ~ *Max Planck, Nobel Prize winning physicist*

■ The quality of your life is a direct function of the quality of questions you ask. Looking for the right answers is only human. Living the great questions is divine.

■ "The reasonable man adapts to the world; the unreasonable one persists in trying to adapt the world to himself. Therefore all progress depends on the unreasonable man." ~ *George Bernard Shaw*

■ We are all in competition with anyone anywhere who does what we do. We're also in partnership with them. There is one global standard against which we're all being measured. Anyone who stretches us to be more than we otherwise would have been without them is a powerful ally.

■ "The World is a book, and those who do not travel read only a page."
~ *Saint Augustine*

■ **See beyond the things that you're used to seeing.** See through the things that get in the way. See the things that others don't see. See more by seeing more things. All judgment is a matter of perspective. All travel enriches your perspective. Get out there.

■ **Be an ambassador for the world.** Pledge allegiance to the planet. Make mobility your model. Participate in your own personal Olympics. Invite others to join you.

■ **"Entrepreneurs are like visionaries.** One of the ways they run forward is by viewing the thing that they are doing as something that is going to be the whole world."
~ Reid Hoffman, Founder of LinkedIn

■ **Talk to other people in their language –** even if you have to use Google translation.

■ **When the sun rises over Africa, the ante-lope knows that it must run faster than the fastest lion if it's to survive.** And when the sun rises over Africa, the lion knows it must run faster than the antelope if it's to eat. So the bottom line is, whoever you are and wherever you are, when the sun rises over Africa, you better start running.

I STUDY:

Decide on the three international affairs you want to learn more about every week. Then study them. Change your three international affairs every week.

I EXPERIENCE:

Discover as many ways as you can to experience other people's cultures. Travel as soon as you can. Reach out to other communities in your geography. Read, listen, watch and learn.

_____

_____

_____

_____

_____

_____

_____

_____

_____

_____

_____

_____

_____

_____

_____

_____

_____

_____

_____

_____

_____

_____

I CONTRIBUTE:

Explore how you can contribute to the world. Upload a video. Make a donation. Join a discussion group. Go on a mission. Make a difference – size doesn' t count.

FINANCIAL WELL-BEING

Feeling of being in control of one's financial situation; grounded optimism about one's financial future; mindset that enables one to pursue one's dreams without being constrained by financial fears; a buffer zone between oneself and desperation; an understanding that wealth is generated by fully actualizing one's talents; personal generosity; faith that if one takes the right steps, and keeps on walking, the rewards will follow.

MANTRA

"I have everything I need to succeed. My real wealth is within me. I will always have enough."

FINANCIAL WELL-BEING

■ **Know the language of money.** Talk is money because money talks. There is a direct correlation between wealth and communication. The more people you talk to, the more they help you make more money.

··

■ **Rich: Abounding in natural resources or qualities; of great value or worth; producing abundantly; plentiful or ample; deep, strong or vivid.** Wealth is always a matter of belief.

··

■ **Capital: Any form of wealth employed or capable of being employed in the production of more wealth.** It is financial, intellectual, social, emotional, cultural, and experiential. Use it or lose it. Be interested in your capital to earn interest on your capital. Capital is that part of wealth which is devoted to obtaining further wealth.

··

■ **Partner: A person associated with others as a principal in a joint venture, sharing its risks and profits.** Build a reputation as someone who becomes rich by making others rich.

··

■ Currency: Something that is used as a medium of exchange; the quality of being widely accepted; something hard; circulated from person to person. A currency is only as valuable as how much people want it. Understand your own currency when you're trading with others.

....

■ Asset: A useful or desirable thing; an item that has a value to others; the opposite of a liability; something that can be converted into cash; a property that generates income. You are your greatest asset. Work on yourself, not just your job.

....

■ Income: Something that comes in to cover what goes out. Your income determines your outcome. We cannot give what we do not have.

....

■ "Those with comprehensive financial plans scored 62 percent higher on emotional well-being than those without, as well as 45 percent higher in overall contentment."
~ *2013 Financial Planning Standards Council Survey*

∙∙∙

■ Be generous at a level that others consider crazy. The more you pay it forward, the greater your payback. It's a beautiful thing in life: we cannot help others without first helping ourselves. If all wealth is a direct reciprocation of the contribution we make to others, generosity is a force multiplier.

∙∙∙

■ The more value we create, the more valuable we become; or rather, the more value-able we become.

∙∙∙

■ Be the cause others rally around because they feel stronger and luckier around you. Become their catalyst for luck, their lightning rod for fortune and the channel to their success. Feed others and you'll eat very well.

∙∙∙

MY MANTRAS

_____

_____

_____

■ **You don't know what you don't know but this is where the miracles happen.** The most important things in our lives happen in our absence. Trust that a miracle is coming soon to a moment near you.

....

■ **Just wanting something doesn't get you what you want.** Action does. Take the first step now.

....

■ **If you put on yellow goggles, at first everything looks yellow. Then you stop even noticing yellow.** What have you stopped noticing? What do you need to notice?

....

MY MANTRAS

_____

_____

_____

_____

_____

_____

_____

_____

_____

_____

_____

_____

_____

- **Financial well-being is your revenue minus your requirements.** Simplify your wants and you'll increase your wealth.

....

- **If you put all your eggs in one basket, take damn good care of the basket.**

....

- **There is no life after debt.** Borrow only to invest in assets that appreciate. Living beyond your means is a one-way ticket to misery. Deficits can finance a country but not an individual. Sooner than later, you'll pay for it.

....

- **A short cut will become your road to ruin.** Make your money by earning it. Any other way is a short-lived bonus that could blow up your life.

....

- **The three ingredients for financial well-being are sweat, imagination and information.**

....

- **Whatever wealth you lose wasn't yours to begin with.** It was simply on loan. If you don't pay attention to it, it will go away.

....

- **The opposite of wealth is worry.** Don't let the fear of losing your money lead to the loss of your talent.

....

■ **Don't bank on things getting better.** Bank on yourself getting better. Your financial well-being will follow your personal growth.

....

■ **An oak tree produces the most acorns between fifty and eighty years old.** The first 50 years are all about preparation.

....

■ **Build your network of wealthy people.** Affluence is created by the communities in which we circulate. The "wealthy" have first-hand knowledge of what it takes to get that way.

....

MY MANTRAS

■ Spend money to save time so you can invest the time in making more money.

....

■ You can pay for all the best financial advice, but it's always your choice where you invest your money. Own the decision. Reap the dividends. Pay the penalties. Blame is the alibi of losers.

....

■ **Money is emotion.** Negative feelings block your financial well-being.

....

■ If the love of money is the root of all evil, the love of your profession is the root of all money. If you do it for the love of it, the money will follow.

....

■ **Money has a different meaning to everyone.** The meaning of money shapes our ability to get more of it. If it means security to you, you'll be too conservative and it will pass you by. If it means contribution to you, you'll multiply your money by giving it away. If it means energy, you'll make more of it by doing more for it. What does it mean to you? Your answer will be the biggest source or obstacle to your financial well-being.

....

■ "Wealth is the ability to fully experience life." ~ *Henry David Thoreau*

....

■ **If you discount your price, others will discount you.** Financial well-being comes at a price. We have to be willing to pay it. And we have to be willing to charge it. You're worth more than you think you are. Have you noticed that great brands never go on sale?

....

■ **Money is the arithmetic of happiness.** It's a multiplier, not a taboo. Talk about it to people who will help you get more of it.

....

■ "In a country well governed, poverty is something to be ashamed of. In a country badly governed, wealth is something to be ashamed of." ~ *Confucius*

....

■ "When wealth is lost, nothing is lost; when health is lost, something is lost; when character is lost, all is lost." ~ *Billy Graham*

....

■ **If you create happiness, you'll create wealth.** Happy people are always wealthy, but wealthy people are not always happy. If you focus on one thing, focus on creating happiness.

....

■ **Don't set out to be wealthy.** Set out to be useful. Wealth is a byproduct of productivity.

....

■ **Don't envy others' wealth.** Envy erodes financial well-being because it eliminates gratitude. Whatever we take for granted gets taken away.

....

■ **Inherited wealth is not what built this country.** True wealth is built by anyone who started with very little.

....

■ **Financial well-being is not a zero-sum game.** It can't happen at someone else's expense. It must happen to their advantage so they become an asset not an enemy. Even if they lose money, they must gain a lesson and keep their self-respect.

....

■ **"It's never been harder to find a job and never been easier—for those prepared for this world—to invent a job or find a customer.** Anyone with the spark of an idea can start a company overnight, using a credit card, while accessing brains, brawn and customers anywhere. The term 'outsourcing' is also out of date. There is no more 'out' anymore. Firms can and will seek the best leaders and talent to achieve their goals anywhere in the world."
~ *Thomas Friedman*

....

MY MANTRAS

■ **Financial well-being is a discipline that requires discipline.** What do I mean? Discipline comes from being a disciple of someone or something. It's a philosophy towards money that drives a strategy around creating financial well-being. At the same time, the philosophy and strategy must be executed rigorously to sustain financial well-being. Financial well-being is dependent on a system that methodically delivers a consistent result. The process must be proven over time. Experiment and explore. Then figure out and fine tune. What's your philosophy and strategy? Mine is: Money is a tool to shape my ideal life. I use it to engage with the best people doing the best things in the world. That's what I've done with this book.

••

■ **No matter how wealthy you may be, act like you are a P.H.D** – Poor, Hungry and Driven.

••

MY MANTRAS

_____

_____

_____

_____

_____

I AM CONFIDENT BECAUSE:

Identify the three reasons why you should be optimistic and confident about your financial future.

I BUILD MY WEALTH BY:

Define your personal strategy for building wealth. Get guidance from people who are wealthy. Overlay their advice with a professional perspective.

MY NEXT STEPS ARE:

Determine the steps you must take today to achieve financial wellbeing. Take the steps. Repeat daily.

I hope you're inspired to take powerful action.

I also hope you'll create your own mantras and share them with the people around you. You never know the impact of a well-timed motivational message. What you do know is that someone, somewhere, is depending on you to help them through a difficult moment.

As you pollinate others' possibilities, they cross-pollinate yours. That's where the nectar is.

Define your moonshot. Email it to me. Maybe we can make it real together. Remember, I am a wizard – just like you. Together, we can achieve amazing things. The world is waiting for it.

Thank you for partnering with me. I love thrilling someone with an idea at just the right time for them. Until the next time, take the next step. It may be a giant leap.

Take your moonshot.
There will never be a
better time than now.

To explore how Mike can help
expand your team's ability
to create amazing results,
call 1.416.917.6007
or email Mike
mike.lipkin@environics.ca